UNDERSTANDING DATA VISUALIZATIONS

DATA GEEK

TYLER HOFF

Published in the United States of America by Cherry Lake Publishing
Ann Arbor, Michigan
www.cherrylakepublishing.com

Series Adviser: Kristin Fontichiaro

Library of Congress Cataloging-in-Publication Data has been filed and is available at catalog.loc.gov

Cherry Lake Publishing would like to acknowledge the work of the Partnership for 21st Century Learning.
Please visit *www.p21.org* for more information.

Printed in the United States of America
Corporate Graphics

ABOUT THE AUTHOR

Tyler Hoff loves libraries. He enjoys playing with good dogs (all dogs are good dogs), cooking, and reading.

TABLE OF CONTENTS

Introduction

Have you ever wondered how to read a confusing map? Or maybe you saw an odd picture on your Instagram timeline. It was not a picture of a pet, food, or sunset. Instead, it was filled with numbers and words, and you didn't know where to start. These kinds of images are called **infographics**.

If you have seen images like this and wondered what they meant, this book is for you! Maps, infographics, charts, and other things that show information visually are called **data visualizations**. Data visualizations are everywhere. They are shared on social media, presented by politicians and journalists, and hung on classroom walls. Even a subway map is a kind of data visualization!

If you've ever used a map to find your way, you've successfully read a data visualization!

Because data visualizations are so popular, we need to know how to read them. Data visualizations can be fun. For example, they can tell you the most popular bands in different states, who cooks the weirdest food on Thanksgiving, and where people like to travel to the most in winter. Many other kinds of important information are contained in visualizations, as well. You might look up directions or weather forecasts using maps. You might look at charts to learn about crime statistics. This book will break down data visualizations and explore what different types do well and not so well. This way, you can easily read confusing data visualizations.

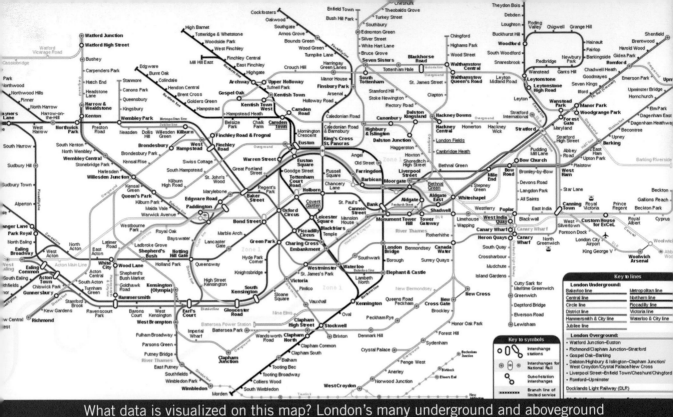

What data is visualized on this map? London's many underground and aboveground public transportation systems. Using colors and special symbols in place of each station and traffic helps us see the system quickly.

Subway Maps

Believe it or not, subways existed for years before anyone made maps for them. The first subway was the London Underground, which opened in 1863. Each train line in the subway system was owned by a different company, and no one wanted to make maps of anyone else's lines. A newspaper called The Evening News created the first map to show all the lines in 1907.

All of these maps tried to show the lines geographically. That means they tried to draw the train lines exactly where they would be in the city. This made it very difficult to show the entire network. It wasn't until 1931 that Harry Beck created the first **diagrammatic** map of the Underground. It only shows the order of the stops on the train lines and where they meet. This is the kind of map still used for most subways today!

CHAPTER 2

Pie Charts

The first kinds of visualizations we will talk about are pie charts. Despite the name, most pie charts don't contain any information about pie. They are called pie charts because they are round and cut into "slices." They are sometimes also called circle charts. This chapter will slice into what pie charts are used for, then bake up some elements to look for when you read a pie chart.

Pie charts are best used to compare parts of a whole. Let's say we have a pumpkin pie. If we cut it into six equal pieces, each piece is one-sixth (17%) of the pie. If we made a chart showing those six pieces, it would have six equal parts. Some pie charts have pieces of equal size, but most do not. Pie charts are also good for comparing fractions of different sizes that are part of the same whole. Let's look at an example!

The pie chart on page 9 shows the favorite pies of 30 kids. There are four options: pumpkin, pecan, apple, and cherry. It is labeled well, so we can easily see which colors represent which pies. We can also see that 40% of the kids (12 of them) like pumpkin, 23% (7) like pecan, 23% (7) like cherry, and 14% (4) picked apple. If we add all those numbers together, the total is 100%. This is what a pie chart is supposed to do!

Even without labels, you can see that apple is the smallest fraction and pumpkin is the largest. This is because the size of the

Why Use Percentages?

Percentages and fractions are two ways of expressing the same thing. One-sixth is the same as 17%. So why use a percentage instead of a fraction? Well, the reason is in the word percent. *Percent comes from the Latin* per centum. *It means "out of every hundred." When someone says 20 percent—or 20%—it means 20 out of 100. Percentages are useful when simplifying big* **denominators**. *For example, as of the 2010* **census**, *37,253,956 people live in California. But a total of 308,745,538 people live in the United States. Those numbers are so big that it is hard to picture them! It is much easier to say that 12.06% of the United States population lives in California.*

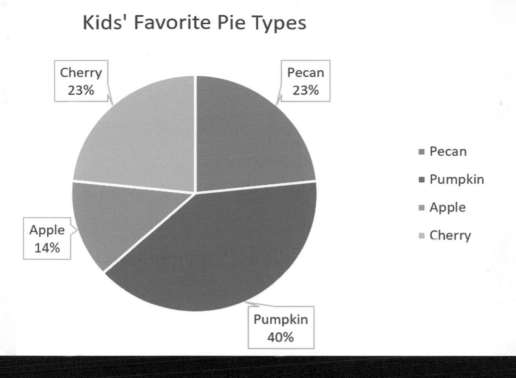

Kids' Favorite Pie Types

Cherry 23%

Pecan 23%

Apple 14%

Pumpkin 40%

- Pecan
- Pumpkin
- Apple
- Cherry

The chart above shows how many kids in a class preferred each type of pie.

slice in a pie chart should reflect the size of the number. However, labels are important in pie charts because it is often hard to see exactly what percentage of a chart something is. For example, in our chart above, it might be hard to tell that cherry and pecan are equally popular without their labels.

Another thing to look out for is how pie charts use color. People who make pie charts like to use colors related to the different slices of the chart. That's why the pumpkin section is orange! However, overly colorful charts can be confusing. So can charts that use very similar colors.

Kids' Orange Juice Preferences

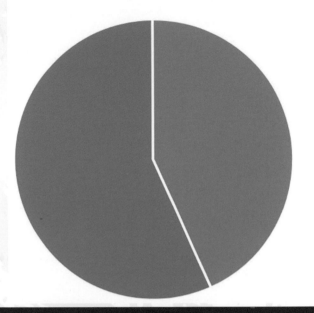

- Orange Juice With Pulp
- Orange Juice Without Pulp

Because the colors here are almost identical, this chart is hard to understand.

The chart above shows the same class of 30 kids. This time it asks what kind of orange juice they like. Thirteen students (43%) chose pulp. Seventeen (or 57%) prefer pulp-free. Both types of orange juice are shown with similar shades of orange. If you just glanced at this pie chart, it would be hard to tell which slice was which!

This gets even more confusing with small slices. The pie chart on the next page shows students' favorite chocolate ice cream flavors. Each color is a different shade of brown. You'll notice that it is very hard to tell which is which.

[21ST CENTURY SKILLS LIBRARY]

Kids' Favorite Kinds of Ice Cream

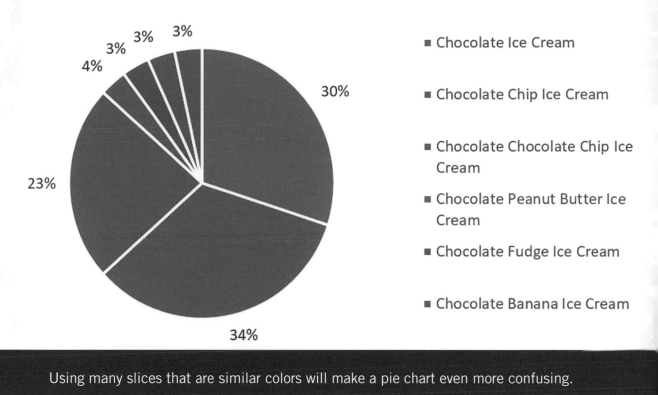

- Chocolate Ice Cream
- Chocolate Chip Ice Cream
- Chocolate Chocolate Chip Ice Cream
- Chocolate Peanut Butter Ice Cream
- Chocolate Fudge Ice Cream
- Chocolate Banana Ice Cream

Using many slices that are similar colors will make a pie chart even more confusing.

The chart on page 12 brings up another potential problem with pie charts: the number of slices they have. Some pie charts have too many slices. This makes a pie chart hard to read because it's hard to tell how large each slice is compared to the others. It is also hard to tell exactly how big a slice is when it is not labeled with a percentage.

Sometimes the chart design makes it hard to know if slices are too big or too small. One way this happens is when someone makes a 3D pie chart. This next one shows students' favorite types of ethnic foods.

Kids' Favorite Ethnic Foods

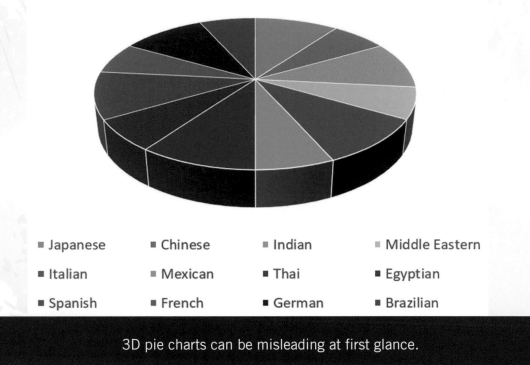

- Japanese
- Chinese
- Indian
- Middle Eastern
- Italian
- Mexican
- Thai
- Egyptian
- Spanish
- French
- German
- Brazilian

3D pie charts can be misleading at first glance.

Just from looking, it might seem like Italian and Thai are the two most popular foods. Those slices of the chart look the biggest. However, they are actually equal to Japanese, Indian, Spanish, and German. They just look bigger because of the 3D effect on the chart.

This chart also has some color problems. Even though the colors on this pie chart are different, there are so many categories that some of them repeat in different shades. This makes it hard to tell the difference between slices.

Rules of Thumb

- Check that your pie chart percentages add up to 100.
- When the colors of a pie chart are very similar, you have to read the labels carefully to understand the chart.
- Be cautious when you see 3D graphics. The 3D effect can make some parts seem larger or smaller than they are.

CHAPTER 3

Bar Charts

In the last chapter, we learned that pie charts are good at showing parts of a whole. Bar charts can do that and a lot more! Bar charts, also called bar graphs, are charts where amounts are measured in bars of different sizes. Normally this kind of chart counts amounts of the same thing in different places, times, or conditions.

Bar charts have an x-axis and a y-axis. The x-axis is the **horizontal** side of the chart. The y-axis is the **vertical** side of the chart. One axis always has lines marking different numbers. The amount between each number is the same each time. That amount is called the **interval**. The other axis shows different categories. Let's look at an example.

Books in Different Rooms

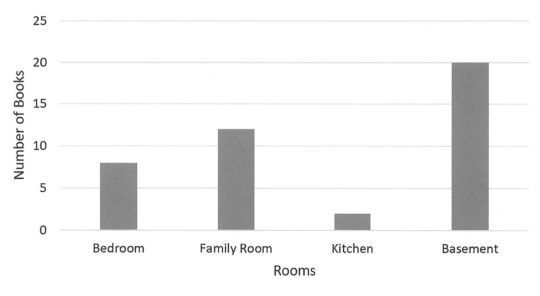

Pay careful attention to the interval used in a bar chart.

In the chart above, the y-axis shows how many books are in each room. The x-axis shows what the different rooms are. This kind of chart makes it easy to see there are a lot of books in the bedroom and family room, but even more in the basement! The interval is five, because the lines are counting by five. This chart is easy to read because the interval was chosen well.

Some charts are confusing because their intervals (the amount of change between each marked line on the y-axis) are the wrong size. Another confusing mistake is when the y-axis starts at an

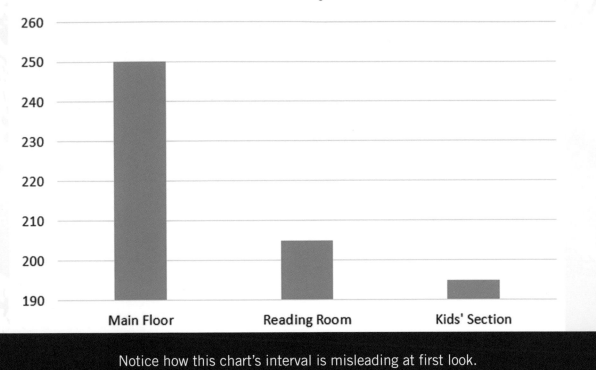

School Library Books

Notice how this chart's interval is misleading at first look.

unexpected point instead of zero. The chart above shows how many books are in the school library.

If you didn't check the y-axis, you might think the main floor had way more books than either the reading room or kids' section. Notice that it starts at 190, not zero. The main floor does have more, but the kids' section still has 195 books! If you didn't check the y-axis, you wouldn't be able to tell. This is a good example of how charts can sometimes be misleading.

When you look at a chart, you should also pay attention to design choices, especially font choices. A font is the way the letters in a piece of writing look. Just like people have different handwriting, sometimes designers choose different fonts.

Fonts can look really cool! Other times, they can be hard to read. Fonts can look like very small cursive or big block writing. Some don't use normal letters at all. Some are designed to make you feel a certain way. For example, some fonts are creepy, while others have the feeling of being old-fashioned. When you look at a bar chart, it is important to be sure you can read the font clearly. You should also make sure the font is not affecting your opinion of what the chart says.

Sometimes chart makers use things other than simple bars like the ones above. For example, a chart might use the outline of

Rules of Thumb

- *Always check how big the interval is on a bar chart.*
- *Think about a chart's design choices. How do the designs make you feel? Do they make the chart hard to read?*

Look at the different fonts on these poster designs. Do you notice how each one gives the poster a different feeling? How might fonts impact the emotions you feel when you see a chart?

a person for a chart on the population of different countries. That's a cool idea! But because of the shape, it could also be hard to read.

Another design choice is to show the bars in 3D. Just like 3D pie charts, these can look great. However, making a chart 3D changes how large the bars look and can accidentally add confusion. This makes it harder to compare different bars on the chart, just like how the pie chart slices looked too big or too small.

More Font Characteristics

There are a few different terms that designers use to describe fonts. The first is weight. *Weight refers to how thick the letters in the font are. Another is* kerning. *This refers to how close together the letters in a font are. One last term is* serif. *Serifs are the little flourishes on the ends of some letters.*

CHAPTER 4

Graphs

Graphs are among the most common kinds of data visualizations. You've probably heard about graphs in math class, but they're useful for all kinds of things. For example, they make it very easy to see how **trends** change over time.

Like bar charts, graphs have an x-axis and y-axis. Unlike bar charts, both axes in a graph count data, like the y-axis on a bar chart. Often you will see graphs that go from a negative number to a positive number on one axis, and sometimes both. This is called the range, the difference between the lowest data point on an axis and the highest.

Data points (or points, for short) are individual points of information on graphs. Points have an x value and a y value. Each represents a different kind of information, depending on the

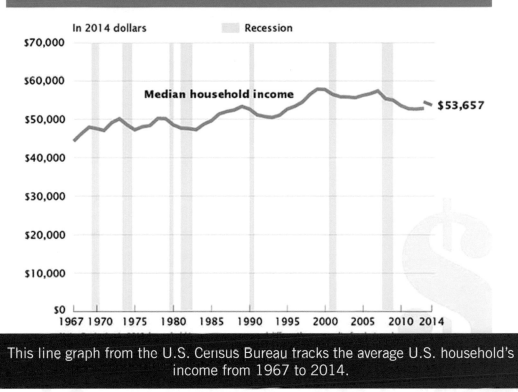

U.S. Income Through the Years
1967 to 2014

In 2014 dollars   ▢ Recession

Median household income

$53,657

This line graph from the U.S. Census Bureau tracks the average U.S. household's income from 1967 to 2014.

graph. Some graphs will show you the individual points. Others will just have a line that tracks the changes between points. Some will show both the specific points and the line. A graph with only a line is called a line graph. A graph that only has points is called a scatter plot. Line graphs are best for showing how things change over time, while scatter plots are best for comparing two types of data. For example, the line graph above shows **median** yearly income for U.S. families over a period of years.

In the line graph above, the x-axis counts years and the y-axis counts dollars. Notice that the x-axis does not start at zero. Graphs

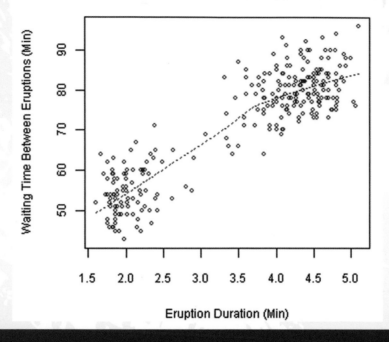

Old Faithful Eruptions

Waiting Time Between Eruptions (Min)

Eruption Duration (Min)

What does this scatter plot tell you about Old Faithful's eruptions?

often only show the parts of the axes that matter. This makes it easier to see trends in the data. But it also means you have to be careful to always check where the axes start! This graph is clearly labeled, and the line is also clearly marked.

A good example of a scatter plot is above. It compares how often Old Faithful (a geyser in Yellowstone National Park) erupts and how long the eruptions last. What does the graph tell you about eruptions? You might notice that eruptions that happen close together do not last as long.

Old Faithful is a geyser named for its reliable eruptions. How do we know they're reliable? Park rangers have collected data for decades!

Rules of Thumb

- Pay attention to where the axes start and end.
- Check the size of the interval.
- Don't assume that either axis begins at zero.

Many people rely on graphs to keep track of their investments.

You can see at a glance that a scatter plot is very different from a line graph. Instead of the single line, there are lots of small dots with another line that does not connect any of the dots. Both axes are well labeled, and the intervals make sense for the range of the data.

As with bar charts, intervals are important for graphs. If intervals are the wrong size, it is easy to think there is no change in data where there is actually a lot of change, or the other way around. One way to tell if the interval is good is to notice whether the space in the graph is being fully used or if it feels cramped.

All graph makers make design choices to best present their data, which means graphs are not always straightforward. As with other data visualizations, color and font choices can make graphs hard to read. Or they can attempt to influence how you feel about the subject of the graph. Most graphs use simple dots to mark data points, but some use images, such as a coin for a graph related to money or TVs for a graph tracking TV-watching habits.

The Stock Market Graph

One famous line graph is based on the stock market. The stock market is very complicated, but a short explanation is that people buy and sell stocks, which are parts of companies. As they do, stock prices go up and down. All of that buying and selling activity is collected. Together, it forms the stock market index, which is presented as a line graph. You can check out this graph at www.macrotrends.net/1319/dow-jones-100-year -historical-chart. Because people have been collecting stock market data for so long, there is a lot of information in this graph. As you look at it, try adjusting the range to see the difference that changing intervals makes.

Infographics

This chapter charts a course through the most complex type of data visualization: infographics. Infographics are a combination of charts and art projects. They show information in a visually interesting way so it catches viewers' eyes. Sometimes infographics show information in fresh and exciting ways. Other times they just make things more difficult to understand. Let's start by charting a course through a common infographic: a U.S. presidential election map!

The map on the next page shows the results of the 2012 presidential election in each state by coloring each state red or blue. If you were not already familiar with U.S. presidential elections, this infographic could be confusing, because it doesn't tell you what the numbers mean (they show the number of votes

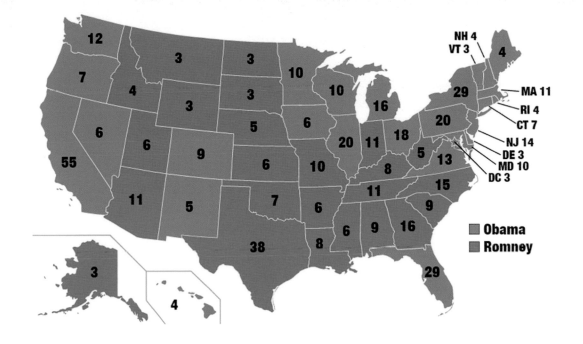

This map shows the results of the 2012 U.S. presidential election.

each state is worth). The different colors and lines between states are clear, although it is a little hard to see the specific states in the Northeast. It would also be hard to figure out which state is which if you didn't already know.

This kind of infographic is fairly straightforward, but there are others that require you to read them in a certain order. One of the first infographics, created by a Frenchman named Charles Minard in 1861, works this way.

This infographic (shown on page 28) starts on the left and traces the path of French leader Napoleon Bonaparte's invasion of

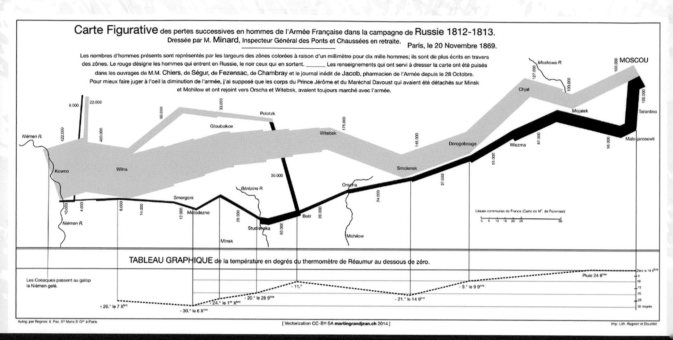

Charles Minard's infographic about Napoleon Bonaparte's invasion of Russia was one of the first infographics. In a single image, he shows troop movements, a map, and the number of troops. Being able to show multiple data stories at once makes this an interesting infographic.

Maps: The Most Common Infographic

Probably the most common infographics are maps. They are designed for many different purposes. Political maps show political information, such as the borders of states and countries. Topographical maps show elevation, or how high the ground is, using lines and colors. We even have maps of the ocean and air, called nautical and aeronautical charts.

Russia. It shows the size of the army, the temperatures over time, and the locations the army passed through. The text is in French, but you can still get the general message. Finding the starting point is central to understanding infographics. The shape of the infographic can help you. If it is square or rectangular, it probably starts in the upper left. If it is a circle, it may start in the center or at the top.

After thinking about where to start reading an infographic, the next step is to ask why it was made. Infographics can be organized into two main categories: informational and persuasive. Informational infographics are created to share information the creator finds interesting. Persuasive infographics are created to convince readers of something. The best way to figure out which category an infographic belongs in is to see who made it.

Rules of Thumb

- *Ask why the infographic was made. What is its purpose?*
- *Ask who made the infographic. What is his or her perspective?*

Many infographics have their creator's name on them. This might be an individual person, a Web site, a magazine, or a newspaper. An infographic usually includes a list of sources. Knowing who created it, as well as where the creator got his or her information, will help you figure out why it was created. For example, if the creator works for a store or company, the infographic could be persuasive. Once you decide which category the infographic belongs to, ask if the design of the infographic is meant to influence your conclusions. Is some important information left out? Are colors being used to make you feel a certain way about the topic? What about fonts? After you are finished reading the infographic, do you feel a strong emotion about it?

These rules can help you figure out any data visualization, whether it's a pie chart, bar chart, graph, or infographic. Think carefully about everything you see. Consider the source and pay careful attention to the data being presented. Soon, you'll be a pro at reading data visualizations!

For More Information

BOOKS

Colby, Jennifer. *Data in Arguments*. Ann Arbor, MI: Ann Arbor, MI: Cherry Lake Publishing, 2018.

Fontichiaro, Kristin. *Creating Data Visualizations*. Ann Arbor, MI: Cherry Lake Publishing, 2018.

WEB SITES

BEAM—Chart Maker
https://beam.venngage.com
This online tool allows you to experiment with making your own charts and graphs, complete with different colors.

U.S. Census Bureau: Topics
www.census.gov/topics.html
Look up official U.S. government data visualizations on a wide variety of topics.

GLOSSARY

census (SEHN-sus) a survey that collects information about the people living in a certain area

data visualizations (DAY-tuh vizh-oo-uhl-ih-ZAY-shuhns) numerical information presented in a chart, graph, or other visual format

denominators (dih-NAH-mih-nay-turz) the bottom numbers in fractions

diagrammatic (dye-uh-gruh-MAH-tik) in diagram form; a diagrammatic map shows the relationship of points instead of their geographic position

horizontal (hor-ih-ZAHN-tul) going from side to side

infographics (in-foh-GRAF-iks) visual images created from many small pieces of data and information

interval (IN-tur-vul) the distance between numbers on the y-axis of a chart

median (MEE-dee-uhn) a way of calculating the average by finding the middle data point

trends (TRENDZ) the general direction or pattern of data points

vertical (VUR-tih-kuhl) going up and down

INDEX